WILD
CATS

Collector Card

Collector Card

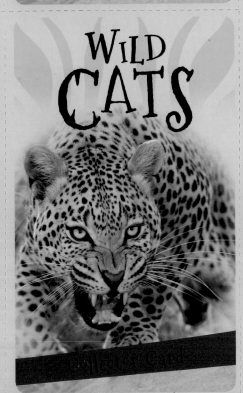

WILD
CATS

Collector Card

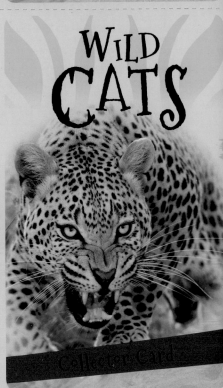

WILD
CATS

Collector Card

Lion

The mighty African predator and king of the savannah lives in prides.

	SCORE
NUMBER IN WILD: approx 20,000	9
BEAUTY:	6
SHOULDER HEIGHT: up to 120 cm	10
HOME RANGE: up to 4532 sq km	10

Jaguar

Powerful big cat of the rainforests and swamps of South America.

	SCORE
NUMBER IN WILD: approx 15,000	7
BEAUTY:	9
SHOULDER HEIGHT: up to 76 cm	4
HOME RANGE: up to 40 sq km	2

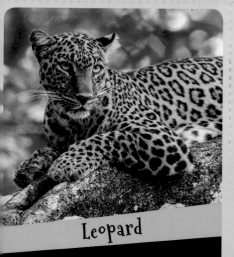

Leopard

Cunning and stealthy tree-climbing big cat of Africa and Asia.

	SCORE
NUMBER IN WILD: approx 20,000	9
BEAUTY:	9
SHOULDER HEIGHT: up to 80 cm	5
HOME RANGE: up to 2182 sq km	8

Cheetah

The fastest land animal – for short bursts – is always on the lookout for danger.

	SCORE
NUMBER IN WILD: less than 10,000	6
BEAUTY:	8
SHOULDER HEIGHT: up to 94 cm	6
HOME RANGE: up to 1642 sq km	7

It's all about…

WILD CATS

KINGFISHER

First published 2017 by Kingfisher
an imprint of Macmillan Children's Books
20 New Wharf Road, London N1 9RR
Associated companies throughout the world
www.panmacmillan.com

Series editor: Sarah Snashall
Design: Wildpixel Ltd
Written by Sarah Snashall

ISBN 978-0-7534-4152-7

9 8 7 6 5 4 3 2 1

1TR/0717/WKT/UG/128MA

A CIP catalogue record for this book is available from the British Library.

Printed in China

Picture credits
The Publisher would like to thank the following for permission to reproduce their material.
Top = t; Bottom = b; Centre = c; Left = l; Right = r.
Cover Shutterstock/Stuart G Porter; back cover iStock/JeffGrabert; Pages 2–3, 30–31 iStock/
ACS15; 4 iStock/rpbirdman; 5t iStock/bas0r; 5 Alamy/Rolf Nussbaumer Photography;
6 iStock/WLDavies; 7t iStock/pjmalsbury; 7b Shutterstock/Jason Prince; 8 iStock/Global P,
iStock/nskynesher; 9t iStock/GlennMason; 9b iStock/julianwphoto; 10–11 Alamy/Mike Hall;
11 Alamy/imageBROKER; 12–13 iStock/jez_bennett; 13 iStock/GP232; 14 iStock/
stefbennett; 15t iStock/FourOaks; 15b Shutterstock/nwdph; 16 iStock/dschaef; 17 Getty/
Winifried Wisniewski; 18–19 Getty/Anup Shah; 19 iStock/Sebastian Lichtenstein; 20 Alamy/
imageBROKER; 21t iStock/davemhuntphotography; 21b iStock/JeffGrabert; 22 iStock/svehlik;
23 iStock/through-my-lens; 24 Shutterstock/Kathrin Hueber; 25t iStock/John Pitcher;
25b iStock/Donyanedomam; 26b Getty/Patrick Aventurier; 27 iStock/CoreyFord;
28–29 Shutterstock/Galina Savina; 28 Getty/Pete Oxford; 32 iStock/Mlenny.
Cards: Front tl iStock/Byrdyak; tr iStock/Trevorplott; bl iStock/girischacf; br iStock/
ivanmateev; Back tl iStock/through-my-lens; tr iStock/RamonCarretero; bl iStock/jocrebbin;
br iStock/Leonardo Prest Mercon Ro

Front cover: A leopard snarls as it stalks its prey.

CONTENTS

Big or small?

There are four roaring big wild cats: the lion, the tiger, the leopard and the jaguar. Other big cats in the wild include the snow leopard and the cheetah, and many small wild cats, such as the clouded leopard, the lynx and the wildcat.

The Siberian tiger is the largest wild cat.

The European wildcat is the direct ancestor of domestic pet cats.

The snow leopard has a thick, furry tail almost as long as its body!

SPOTLIGHT: Snow leopard

Shoulder height:	up to 60 cm
Number in wild:	fewer than 8000
Conservation status:	endangered
Lives:	Himalayas, China, Russia

Family life

Lions live in family groups, but most other wild cats live on their own. A female will look after her cubs until they are up to two years old. She teaches them to hunt and protects them from predators, such as hyenas.

When a mother cleans her cubs she forms strong family bonds.

FACT...

Cats have a large 'home range',
which they mark with their scent.

A mother cheetah hides her cubs
in the grass while she hunts.

Killing machines

A cat's body is powerful and fast. It is well
suited to finding, chasing and killing prey

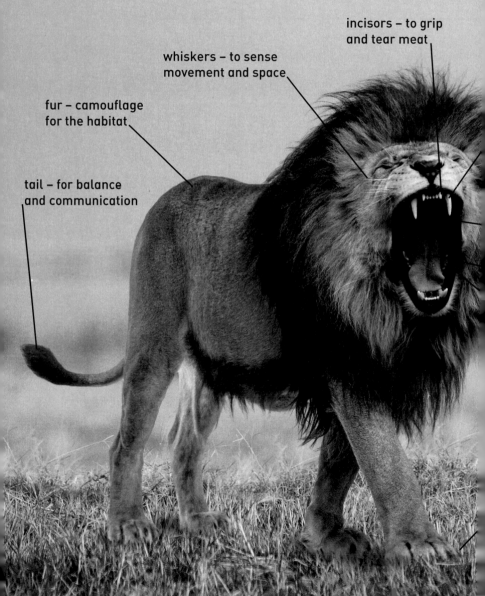

incisors – to grip
and tear meat

whiskers – to sense
movement and space

fur – camouflage
for the habitat

tail – for balance
and communication

Lions, tigers, leopards and jaguars have a specially developed voice box that allows them to roar.

canines – to rip and tear meat

ears – for excellent hearing

Jacobson's organ (in mouth) – to 'taste' the air

rough tongue – to scrape meat from bones

carnassials – to cut meat

dewclaw – fifth toe for holding down prey

The serval can leap high into the air to catch birds.

The largest cats

Most wild tigers live in protected areas in India but they also live in forests in Russia and in jungles across Asia. Tigers usually hunt alone at night. They silently creep up on their prey before pouncing and grabbing it by the throat.

FACT...

A tiger can be recognized by its stripes – every tiger has a different pattern of stripes.

Tigers are excellent swimmers and bathe to keep cool.

A Siberian tiger can be over three metres long.

SPOTLIGHT: Siberian tiger

Shoulder height:	up to 120 cm
Number in wild:	300
Conservation status:	endangered
Lives:	Siberia, Manchuria

11

King of the cats

Lions are the second largest wild cats. Most lions live on the African savannah in family groups called prides. The female lions hunt for food while the male lions protect the cubs and the rest of the pride. A lion's roar can be heard from almost eight kilometres away.

Lion cubs learn to hunt by watching other adult lions and practising on their parents!

FACT...

You can tell the age of a lion by the colour of its nose. A lion's nose starts pink and gradually becomes black as the lion grows old.

Lions hunt together in a group.

Hunter of the Americas

The jaguar, the biggest wild cat in the Americas, stalks its prey almost silently before pouncing. Sometimes jaguars climb trees to wait for prey such as deer and monkeys.

FACT...

The name 'jaguar' means 'he who kills with one leap'.

A panther is a jaguar or a leopard that has been born with black fur, but you can still see the pattern of its fur underneath.

A male jaguar hunts across a home range that might have female jaguars living in it. He will protect the area and the females from other male jaguars.

The jaguar's spots are solid on its neck and head but rosette-shaped on its body.

Jaguars like to swim, hunting river animals such as fish, turtles and even caimans!

Powerful cats

Leopards are strong and powerful
and can pull a kill twice as heavy as
their own body up a tree. Leopards are
not fussy – they will eat almost anything,
including monkeys and porcupines.

A leopard will climb
a tree to rest or to
ambush its prey.

Leopards live in grasslands, scrubland, woods and rainforests. Most live in Africa but there are rare leopards in Russia, India and other parts of Asia.

FACT...

A leopard's roar is a series of grunts that sound like wood being cut with a saw.

A leopard can jump six metres forwards and three metres vertically.

The fastest cats

Cheetahs are the fastest land animals in the world. They can sprint across open grassland at up to 120 kilometres an hour, covering over six metres in a single stride.

FACT...

Cheetah cubs have long hair, which fools predators into thinking they are fierce honey badgers.

Cheetahs have fur with solid brown spots and a 'tear track' pattern under their eyes to reduce glare from the sun.

Cheetahs stand on small mounds to keep a look-out for prey and predators.

Built for speed, cheetahs are not as strong as other big cats.

The ocelot lives in the rainforests of Central and South America.

Small and deadly

There are 32 different types of small cat across the world, such as the ocelot, the lynx and the bobcat, which lives in different habitats across the United States.

These smaller wild cats belong to a different family from the big cats, but they are also expert solitary hunters.

FACT...

The Pallas' cat is a prehistoric cat – it's been around for 10 million years!

The margay runs up and down trees like a squirrel, and can hang from a branch by one foot.

A cat with many names

The puma has an amazing number of names – 40! They include cougar, mountain lion, panther and catamount. Pumas are found from Canada to South America and live in a range of habitats, from deserts to forests and mountains.

Pumas are born with spotted fur.

Pumas are the second biggest wild cat found in the Americas (after the jaguar) and the largest of the small cats. They hunt a variety of animals, from insects to adult deer.

A puma has strong back legs to help it leap.

SPOTLIGHT: Puma

Shoulder height: up to 90 cm
Number in wild: about 40,000
Conservation status: not endangered
Lives: American mountains, forests

Lynxes and bobcats

Lynxes are cats with patterned fur and tufted ears. They live in high remote forests across North America, as well as parts of Europe, Central Asia and Russia.

Scientists think the tufts on a lynx's ear help it hear better.

A lynx is about twice the size of a domestic cat. It has spotted fur and longer hair under its chin like a beard.

The Canadian lynx has large padded paws for walking on snow.

The bobcat is a type of lynx that lives in North America.

25

Prehistoric cats

Thousands of years ago giant cheetahs, huge jaguars and fearsome sabre-toothed cats roamed the world.

One of the oldest paintings in the world is of cave lions – an extinct relative of modern lions.

FACT...

Smilodon fossils have been found in prehistoric tar pits. The Smilodon came to eat prey trapped in the tar – and became stuck itself!

One sabre-toothed cat was the Smilodon,
which had two knife-like teeth about
28 centimetres long!

SPOTLIGHT: Smilodon

Shoulder height:	up to 120 cm
Number in wild:	extinct
Conservation status:	extinct
Lived:	North and South America

27

Cats in danger

Sadly, the number of cats living in the wild is falling. Some are killed to make traditional medicines; others are killed by farmers when protecting their cattle. But most die because their habitats are disappearing.

FACT...

More tigers live in captivity than in the wild.

There are only about 300 Iberian lynxes left in the wild.

Across the world zoos, wildlife charities and governments are working together to protect wild cats.

The Amur leopard is one of the most endangered animals in the world.

SPOTLIGHT: Amur leopard

Shoulder height:	up to about 78 cm
Number in wild:	70
Conservation status:	critically endangered
Lives:	Russian forests

GLOSSARY

ancestor A relative from the distant past.

captivity Being held in a secure place and unable to leave.

conservation status Whether an animal is in danger of becoming extinct.

endangered At risk of becoming extinct.

extinct No animals of the species are left alive.

habitat The natural home of an animal or plant.

home range The area where an animal lives and hunts.

Jacobson's organ An organ found in many animals that allows them to smell other creatures.

predator An animal that hunts other animals for food.

prehistoric The time before human written records began.

prey An animal that is hunted by another animal for food.

pride A family of lions.

remote Very far from cities or towns.

rosettes Patterns that look like circles.

sabre-toothed Describes a prehistoric cat with very long teeth. A sabre is a slightly curved sword.

savannah An open grassy plain with only a few trees.

scrubland A dry area with low bushes and grass.

solitary Spends most of its time alone.

tar pits Deep pools of tar (a very sticky liquid that becomes a soft black rock when cold).

INDEX

bobcats 20, 25

bodies 5, 8, 9, 10, 13, 15, 16, 24, 25

catamounts *see* pumas

cheetahs 7, 18–19, 26

cougars *see* pumas

cubs 6, 7, 13, 14, 18, 22

endangered animals 28–29

European wildcats 5

family life 6–7

fossils 26

fur 8, 14, 19, 22, 24, 25

habitats 10, 16, 20, 22, 24, 28

home range 7, 15

hunting 6, 7, 8, 10, 12–13, 14, 15, 17, 23

Iberian lynxes 28

jaguars 14–15, 26

leopards 4, 5, 16–17, 29

lions 6, 8–9, 12–13, 26

lynxes 20, 24–25, 28

margays 21

mountain lions *see* pumas

ocelots 20

Pallas' cats 21

panthers *see* pumas or jaguars

prehistoric cats 26–27

pumas 22–23

roaring 4, 9, 12, 17

sabre-toothed cats 26–27

servals 9

Siberian tigers 11

Smilodon 26–27

snow leopards 4, 5

swimmers 11, 15

teeth 8, 9, 27

tigers 10–11, 28

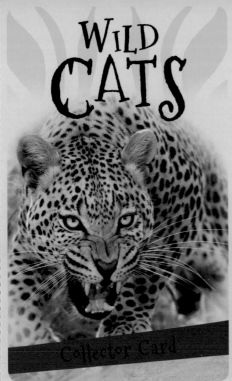

WILD CATS

Collector Card

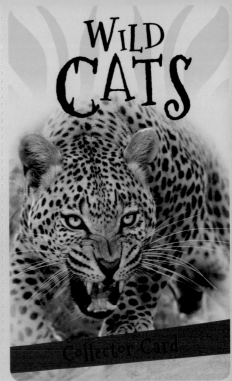

WILD CATS

Collector Card

WILD CATS

Collector Card

WILD CATS

Collector Card

Snow leopard

Solitary, rare and mysterious cat that lives in high Asian mountains.

SCORE

NUMBER IN WILD: fewer than 8000   5
BEAUTY: 7
SHOULDER HEIGHT: 60 cm   2
HOME RANGE: 140 sq km   4

Ocelot

The dwarf leopard of South America is swift on land, in trees and in water.

SCORE

NUMBER IN WILD: more than 40,000   10
BEAUTY: 6
SHOULDER HEIGHT: up to 50 cm   1
HOME RANGE: up to 43 sq km   3

Tiger

Shere Khan in *The Jungle Book* is based on the deadly Bengal tiger.

SCORE

NUMBER IN WILD: about 3800   3
BEAUTY: 10
SHOULDER HEIGHT: 120 cm   10
HOME RANGE: up to 400 sq km   5

Iberian lynx

Bearded, tufted and critically endangered but back from the brink of extinction.

SCORE

NUMBER IN WILD: 400   1
BEAUTY: 4
SHOULDER HEIGHT: up to 70 cm   3
HOME RANGE: unknown   1

Collect all the titles in this series!

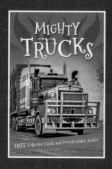

BEASTLY BUGS
DEADLY DINOSAURS
EPIC EXPLORERS
EXOTIC EGYPTIANS

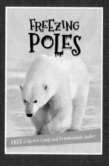

FANTASTIC FLIERS
FAST CARS
FREEZING POLES
GLORIOUS GREEKS

MIGHTY TRUCKS
REMARKABLE ROMANS
RIOTOUS RAINFORESTS
RUSHING RIVERS

FREE Collector Cards and Downloadable Audio!